Bible
Stories

Selected for 7-8 year olds

Retold by
Diane Walker

Illustrated by Julia Pearson

ABINGDON PRESS
Nashville

Preface

There are ten stories in this selection, specially chosen for children aged 7-8.

The story *In the beginning* shows us that God is creative and made people to be his friends.

In *Gideon, the frightened leader* we see that God knows us and loves us just as we are.

The story of the lost son reminds us that God longs to forgive anyone who asks him.

Each one of these stories shows us something of what God is like.

Contents

In the beginning

Before time began, God was here. There was no one else, just God. But God had a plan. He looked at the emptiness and darkness, and out of them he made space, and the earth, spinning silently.

Then he said, "Let there be light!" And light blazed out. God divided it from the darkness, and earth had its first day and night.

Earth hung in space, covered in deep waters. God separated the waters. Some he trapped in clouds and mist in the sky.

Then God gathered together the water left on the earth into oceans, rivers and streams. So the dry land appeared: but it was bare. God commanded it to be clothed in green. Plants and trees sprang up everywhere. God was pleased.

Next, God created the burning sun, the moon and thousands of stars, to light the day and night and show the passing of time. Night came, lit for the first time by moon and stars.

"Now earth is ready for sea-life and for birds," God said. He created all the sizes and shapes he could think of. Earth's silence was shattered as whales, dolphins and birds sang to each other and to God. "Everything is good," God thought.

Then God made all sorts of animals to live on the land; large and small, striped and spotted, quiet and noisy – he was pleased with them all.

"Now everything is ready for my special friends," God said. "They alone will be like me,

able to love and talk with me." And God made
man and woman, Adam and Eve.

Then God rested from the work he had done.

God made a special garden for Adam and Eve. "Live here as my friends," God told them. "You have all you need. You can eat fruit from any of the trees in the garden – except this one. If you eat the fruit of this tree, you will no longer be my friends, and you will die."

Now the serpent was the most cunning animal. He wanted to hurt God and Adam and Eve. He lied to Eve, "The fruit from this tree will make you as great as God himself. That's why he told you not to eat it. Why don't you try some? Of course it won't kill you."

Eve picked some fruit. If this was true, why shouldn't they eat it? She ignored what God had said. Eve bit the fruit, and it tasted good. "Look, Adam," she said, "It's delicious. You try it, too." And Adam took a bite.

Immediately, for the first time, they knew they had done wrong. They felt shame and unhappiness. When God came to talk with them that evening, they hid. God knew what had happened. "You have eaten that fruit, haven't you?" he asked.

Adam said, "It was Eve – she made me!"

God looked at Eve. "No, it wasn't me!" she cried. "The serpent – it's his fault!"

How sad God was! His friends had disobeyed him and now they were lying about it. "Adam and Eve," God said sadly, "you can no longer live here. We can no longer be friends in the same way. This thing you have done is like a wall between us. You must leave the garden. Life will be hard for you from now on."

God watched them walking miserably away. But God still loved them, and he already had a plan to bring them back to him.

God keeps his promises

It was very hot. Abraham sat outside his tent. He shaded his eyes with his hands and looked around at the countryside. It was good land, beautiful and rich, growing strong crops. Many people could live here comfortably, build their houses and graze their herds and flocks. Long ago, God had promised Abraham that one day his family would live in this land in safety and in peace.

God had made Abraham another promise, too. "Look at the stars in the sky, sparkling there in their thousands. You will have as many descendants as there are stars," God had told him. So Abraham had left his comfortable home. He and his wife, Sarah, had packed up their belongings, gathered their herds and, with their servants, had begun their journey.

"And here we are," Abraham thought, "still travelling from place to place through other people's land, living in tents, driving our animals on to find fresh grass. We still have no land of our own on which to live. We have been hungry and tired, frightened and alone. And Sarah and I still have no child of our own. But I believe that God will keep his promises – even though they seem impossible."

As he looked out over the land, Abraham caught sight of three men walking towards him along the dusty track. He hurried to meet them.

"Welcome!" he said. "You must be tired and hot. Come over to my tent and rest."

He sat them in the shade of the trees next to his tent, and brought them water to wash their feet. He and Sarah quickly prepared a meal, and Abraham watched as they ate and drank.

In the tent, Sarah was curious about these three men. Who were they? What did they want? She crept over to the door of the tent, where she could hear what they were saying.

9

"Nine months from now," she heard one of them say, "you and Sarah will have a son."

From her hiding place, Sarah laughed to herself. What a silly thing to say! "I am far too old to have a baby," she thought.

She was startled to hear the man say, "Why did Sarah laugh when I said that? Why does she think she is too old? Doesn't she know that God can do anything?"

Then Sarah realized that the message came from God. She was frightened, and hurried outside. "I didn't really laugh," she said.

"Yes, you did. But it's all right," they reassured her. "Soon you will have a baby boy to care for. He will be part of your great family."

Abraham smiled at his wife. He knew how Sarah felt. He was remembering the time when he too had laughed at God's promise. But he had learned to trust God since then.

A year later, Abraham once more sat outside his tent on a hot, dusty day. He had moved camp many times since God had sent him three special visitors. He still had to stay on other people's land. But Abraham could see all around him the land promised to him.

As he looked at the countryside, he could hear his son crying, and Sarah singing as she rocked the baby to sleep.

"Isaac," Abraham said quietly, "our son Isaac. The son we thought we could not have. One day, this whole land will belong to our family. For God has promised it to us. And God always keeps his promises."

11

Gideon, the frightened leader

God's people were in trouble. They had been worshipping false gods instead of the true and living God. And now, the strong army from the land of Midian kept attacking them, killing and destroying, stealing their food. Some of them even had to live in caves.

On one small farm, a young man called Gideon was threshing his family's wheat. But instead of working out in the open, where the wind would blow away the chaff, he was working inside the winepress. He was hiding from the Midianites. Suddenly, he was not alone: God was there!

"Gideon!" said God. "I want you to defeat the Midianites!"

Gideon was horrified. How could he do that? He was only a young man, from a poor family.

"I will be with you," said God. "I will help you."

So Gideon called together the army. There were 32,000 men. But Gideon was still worried. "Please prove that you really will help me," he asked God. "Every morning, the dew covers everything. Tomorrow morning, let this sheepskin be soaked with dew – but let all the ground around it be dry."

God understood how worried Gideon was. So, in the morning, the sheepskin was wet. The ground around was dry.

But Gideon was still not sure. What would happen to him if he attacked the Midianites – and God did not help him? So he pleaded, "Don't be angry, God. Tonight, do the opposite from last night. Let the ground be soaked with dew, but the sheepskin remain dry. Then I shall be convinced that you will help me."

And, in the morning, there was the sheepskin, completely dry on the wet ground!

Then Gideon led out his army. But God had another shock for him. "Gideon," he said, "there are too many soldiers here. If they win, they will say that they, not God, defeated the Midianites. My people have forgotten how I love and care for them. I must show them this once more. Tell any men who are frightened that they can return home."

To Gideon's horror, 22,000 men gladly hurried home. Now he had only 10,000 men! But God had not finished. "There are still too many men! Take the men to drink at the river. Watch them carefully. Keep only those who drink the water from their cupped hands."

Gideon looked around. Only 300 men were drinking like that! The others put their faces down to the water.

That night, as Gideon lay in the camp with his tiny army around him, he heard God once more. "Listen, Gideon, I know how frightened you are. Go to the Midianites' camp. What you hear there will make you feel better."

So Gideon crept over to the camp. There, he heard men describing their dreams. God had sent them dreams in which Gideon defeated them. Gideon realized that the great army was afraid of him! How patient and thoughtful God had been. Now Gideon was ready to fight.

Quickly he woke his men. He gave each of them a trumpet and a jar holding a flaming torch. He explained his plan.

Then they crept into position round the enemy's camp. At Gideon's signal, they blew on their trumpets and smashed their jars, letting the light stream out. They shouted loudly, "A sword for God and for Gideon!" And the enemy panicked. In the confusion of noise and light, the Midianites attacked each other, and then ran away.

God had saved his people, and Gideon had learned that he could trust God to keep his promises.

God has plans for Ruth

Hundreds of years before Jesus was born in Bethlehem, a woman named Naomi lived there. Her life had not been easy or happy.

Years before, a famine had forced her family to go to live in another country where they could find food. Then, one by one, her husband and later her two sons had died there. So she decided to return to Bethlehem: the famine was now over, and she wanted to live in her real home again. Only one of her daughters-in-law, Ruth, wanted to come to Bethlehem with her.

Naomi warned Ruth how difficult life would be in Bethlehem, but Ruth would not return to her parents' house. "I will never leave you," she said. "I have made my home with you.

Wherever you live, I will live. Your people will be my people, and I will love and follow your God."

Now, life was very hard for the two women. They lived at a time when women could not earn money to support themselves. With no husbands, brothers, or sons to protect them and work for them, they were poor and short of food.

It was harvest-time. Out in the fields, the workers were busy, cutting the wheat and beating out its grain to store as seed for next year or to make into flour. Ruth joined the other poor people who were allowed to search the fields for any grain the workers had left. She and Naomi needed all the grain she could find. It was hot, hard work.

Boaz, the owner of the field in which Ruth was working, watched her. He had not seen her before. He asked his servant who she was. When he found out how she was helping Naomi, he spoke to her. "Help yourself to food and water, and work in my fields again," he said. He told his servants to look after her, and even to drop some grain on purpose for her to find.

Ruth went home very happy that night. She showed Naomi how much grain she had found, and told her about Boaz's kindness. Naomi smiled. "He is our relative," she said. "I am glad you have found someone to look after you."

Ruth returned to Boaz's fields. Boaz watched her and talked with her. Soon he realized that he loved Ruth, and he asked her to marry him.

Now life was good for Naomi and Ruth. Soon, Ruth had a son, Obed. Naomi and Ruth were happy again.

They would have been even happier if they had known what was going to happen. For Obed had a son called Jesse, and Jesse became the father of Israel's greatest king, David. Hundreds of years later, in that same little town, another baby boy was born into this same family. That baby was Jesus.

Life had been difficult for Ruth and Naomi, and they had dreaded the future. But God was carefully planning all the time to make them part of Jesus' family.

The people choose their God

For three years, no rain had fallen on the land of Israel. The plants had died and the soil turned into dust. This was because King Ahab and Queen Jezebel had led the people to worship the false god Baal, instead of the true God.

The prophet Elijah, God's messenger, had been in hiding for these three years, kept safe by God. King Ahab wanted to kill him for bringing God's message. "No rain will fall until the people realize that I am the true God," God had said.

But now it was time for God's prophet Elijah to challenge the prophets of Baal. He stood on Mount Carmel, facing Baal's 450 prophets, in front of all the people.

"Listen! You must decide today whom you will follow – God or Baal. We will ask them both to send down fire on to these altars. Then we will see who is the true God!"

So Baal's prophets tried. All day, they begged Baal to send fire. All day they danced and shouted. But no fire came.

At last, Elijah prepared God's altar. He ordered the people to dig a ditch all around it, and to empty jar after jar of water over it. The water even filled the ditch. "No fire will burn that!" the people muttered.

Then Elijah prayed: "Lord God, show these people that you are God. Send down fire!"

And fire came. It blazed on the altar, burning so fiercely that the stones crumbled and the water in the ditch boiled away.

And the people cried, "This is the true God! We will obey him!"

Then Elijah said, "God is even now sending the rain to you: but these prophets of Baal must die."

When Queen Jezebel heard what had
happened, she threatened to kill Elijah. So he
ran away, hiding in a cave on Mount Horeb.
Then God spoke to him.

"What is the matter, Elijah? Why are you here?"

"I've had enough of being your messenger,
Lord," Elijah complained. "I'm the only one left
who follows you – and all it ever brings me is
danger!"

God understood. "Listen," he said, "for I am
coming to speak with you."

Immediately, a great wind struck the mountain. Rocks shattered and crashed down. Then an earthquake rumbled through the ground, and fire blazed all around. God's power thundered out all around him. But God was not there.

Then Elijah heard a voice, a quiet, loving whisper: "Elijah, you are not alone! Many people in Israel still love me, as you do. And Elisha will be your friend and helper from now on."

Then Elijah remembered how God had fed him during the drought. He realized that God had never stopped caring for him, and would always look after him. So Elijah returned to his work, knowing that God was there with him.

The little girl who helped Naaman

When Elijah had been taken up into heaven, his friend Elisha carried on his work as God's prophet, bringing messages from God to his people, the Israelites. Israel was often at war with other countries. Sometimes, Israelites were captured by their enemies and taken to live as servants in other countries. One of these was a little girl from Israel, who had been taken to live in Syria.

She worked in the house of a famous soldier called Naaman, who commanded the king's army. Sometimes servants were treated cruelly, but the people in Naaman's house were kind to the little girl. She enjoyed helping Naaman's wife to bathe and dress, and to look after the house.

One day, she realized that Naaman and his wife were unhappy. She found out that Naaman had an illness called leprosy which no one at the time could cure. He had white patches and sores all over his skin, and it was getting worse. Soon, he would have to leave his job and his family. No wonder he and his wife were miserable! The little girl wished that she could help. They had always been kind to her. This was her home too, now.

Then she remembered something! She hurried to her mistress.

"Listen!" she said excitedly. "In Israel there is a prophet – a man who does God's work. I am sure he could help Naaman. He has done many wonderful things."

It was worth trying. No one else could help Naaman. The king agreed. Naaman set off for Israel with rich gifts for the prophet. And Naaman's wife and the little girl waited in Syria.

How long the wait seemed! Then, at last, Naaman's chariot pulled up outside. His wife and the servants rushed out: was he cured?

Naaman's happy face and healthy brown skin gave them their answer. He was healed! They crowded round, wanting to hear everything.

"Elisha the prophet didn't even come out of his house to see me! He just sent a message, telling me to dip myself seven times in their River Jordan!" Naaman told them. "I was horrified! How dare he treat me like that! I drove off in my chariot. But my servants showed me I was wrong. If Elisha had asked me to do something brave, I would have done it. It was just my pride stopping me.

"So I went back and bathed seven times – just as he had said – and I was healed! I had quite a long talk with Elisha then. He refused to take any payment. God is very wonderful – and he cares for each of us. I am so glad that I have found out about him: I am going to worship him from now on."

Naaman and his wife were very grateful to the little girl who had shown them what to do. And the little girl thanked God that she had been able to help, and that Naaman now knew about God and wanted to serve him as she did.

A Savior is born

The woman pushed open the door. "It's only where we keep the animals," she said, "but you did say you'd tried everywhere else."

"We have. The town's so crowded." The man turned to the young wife he was supporting with his arm. "Will this be all right?" he asked.

Mary looked at the cave in the flickering lamplight. "Yes, Joseph," she said. "We will stay here. The baby will be born soon."

The woman left them. Joseph gathered hay into a rough bed in the most sheltered corner. He helped Mary to lie down and covered her with his cloak. "Try to rest for a while," he said. Looking round, he caught sight of the animals' feeding trough. He brought it over to her, and filled it with hay. "That will keep the draughts away," he thought. He looked down at Mary. She was so young and tired. He wanted her to be safe and warm in their own little home, not here, miles away in Bethlehem, in an animals' shelter. But they – and all the other strangers packed into the little town – had to obey the Emperor's order to register here.

"God knows all about it," Joseph thought. "He is looking after us." He settled down to wait. Hours later, he was holding Mary's newly born son.

Out on the hillside, above the town, drowsy shepherds were startled awake by a bright,

dazzling light flooding their little camp. Angels, God's messengers, had been sent with urgent, joyful news. "Don't be frightened," they told the shepherds. "Listen! Down in Bethlehem, a baby has been born – a special baby, God's own son, the Savior. He is now sleeping in a manger, an animals' feeding trough. Go to him!"

Then the angels sang a great song of praise to God, which echoed round the hills. Suddenly the song ended: the shepherds were alone once more in the cold, dark night. They hurried down into the town. They soon found the right place, and there they knelt in front of this tiny baby whose birth had brought joy even to the angels. Then the shepherds left, hurrying to tell friends and family about this extraordinary night.

"Even here, miles from home, God sent someone to welcome his son," Mary said to Joseph as they settled down.

Unknown to them, other visitors were on their way, too. But theirs was a long, difficult journey. It was many weeks before they, too, arrived in the little town.

The strangers stood in the busy street outside the small house. "So this is where he is," one said, "after all this time."

"Hardly a palace!" another laughed.

Joseph let them in, and they gazed in amazement at the young child on Mary's knee. So this was the great king God had told them about when he sent them far from their own lands. They followed the brilliant star that had been sent to guide them, and they had brought presents, costly gifts that puzzled Mary and Joseph. For they brought gold for a king and incense for God – for Jesus was both of these. And they brought myrrh, too. For Jesus would die a special death, even though he was also God.

The strangers went away, leaving the family alone. Mary had Jesus to care for, and now she had so many things to think about.

The story of the lost son

Jesus travelled through the country, telling people about the way God wanted them to live and healing those who were sick. He often told interesting stories to help them understand more about God – stories about farmers and animals, servants and robbers. Jesus told this story to show that God wants everyone to be his friends.

There was once a farmer who had two sons. The elder son worked hard for his father, but the younger son was bored.

"I don't want to work here all my life," he thought. So he said to his father, "When you die, Dad, I know I will get some of your money. Give it to me now, so that I can leave this place."

His father was upset because he loved his sons and wanted them both at home with him. But he realized that this son would not be happy staying on the farm.

So he gave him the money, and watched sadly as he packed his bags and left.

The boy was happy. Now, at last, he could enjoy himself! He set up home in a distant town. He bought new clothes.

"I could never wear anything like this on the farm," he laughed. He feasted on the best food, and held noisy, expensive parties. Suddenly, he was very popular! "This is the life," he thought.

But soon, his money ran out. His new friends only liked him for his money, so they left him. Now the son had nothing: no friends, no money, no family.

What should he do? He couldn't even buy food. And then, to make matters worse, there was a famine in the land, so no one had enough to eat. The only job he could get was looking after pigs. His clothes were soon dirty and ragged, and he was always hungry. "Even the pigs are better fed than me!" he moaned.

One day, he could bear it no longer. "I've been stupid," he thought. "I'll go back to Dad. I'll tell him I'm sorry, and that I don't deserve to live as his son. But I'll ask him to give me a job on the farm, for our servants live better than this!" So he set off, hungry, weak and unhappy. "I won't be surprised if Dad refuses even to see me, " he thought.

What a long way it seemed. On and on he trudged. Then, as he stumbled along the dusty road, he saw someone in the distance, running towards him. He shaded his eyes: it looked like his father! But no, it couldn't be... Then he was sure it was his father, hurrying to meet him! He stopped in astonishment – and his father rushed up to him, throwing his arms around him.

"At last!" he said. "You're home! I so wanted you to come home that I've been looking for you every day."

His son stepped back. "Listen, Father. I'm so sorry. I was selfish and wrong. I don't deserve to live as your son again."

"Don't say anything else," his father told him. "Come on! We'll hold a party tonight!" The father told his servants to help his son wash and dress in new clothes. And to show that he was taking the boy back into his family, he ordered, "Put rings on his fingers and sandals on his feet."

"God is like this father," said Jesus. "God longs for each of you to come to him, so that he can treat you as a member of his family. God will welcome you whatever you have done."

A day of miracles

For the past few months, Jesus had been travelling round Galilee. Already many people had heard of him and the wonderful things he had done. Large crowds often followed him, hoping to see more miracles or to hear his wise teaching. Today he had spent hours sitting on the hillside teaching hundreds of people about God, explaining how they could live as God's friends.

At last, he stood up and began to walk down to Capernaum where some of his disciples lived. He was very tired, but the crowds were still following him. Then a man on the edge of the crowd shouted to him. The other people moved away from him hurriedly, for this man had a skin disease which no doctor then could cure. They believed it was easy to catch the disease from each other, so no one wanted to be near him!

"Lord," the man said, "please help me. I believe that you can heal me, if only you would."

Jesus nodded. "I can heal you, and I do want to." He touched the man and said, "You are healed! Show your priest that you are healed, and go back to your family."

The man hurried off, and Jesus walked on to Peter's house, where he was looking forward to a meal and a rest. But he was stopped again! A Roman soldier came up to him.

"Jesus," he began, "my servant is ill at home. Please help him." Jesus agreed to come immediately, but the soldier said, "There is no need. Just command that he should be well – here and now – and I know that he will be. I am a centurion: I give orders and know that they will be obeyed. You have far greater power; a word from you is enough."

Jesus was amazed. This man really understood who he was and believed in him. "Go home," he told the centurion. "Because you believe in me, your servant is already healed." And when the centurion reached home, he found the man completely well.

When Jesus arrived at Peter's house, he found that Peter's mother-in-law was ill. He knelt down beside her and touched her hand. Immediately she felt better. She got up straight away and gave Jesus and his friends a good meal.

But before Jesus had finished eating, a great crowd had gathered at the door. They had brought their ill friends and relatives with them. Jesus walked among them, healing all of them. But he was so tired. How was he to rest?

Jesus told his disciples to take him to the other side of the lake in one of their fishing boats. It was quiet there. He often went up into the hills to talk to God. He climbed into the boat and fell asleep straight away.

Without warning, a sudden storm blew up. The wind roared about the boat, and the waves rose higher and higher. Some of these disciples were fishermen, used to the sudden storms on the lake, but now they panicked! One of them struggled over to wake Jesus.

"Lord, don't you care if we all drown?" they accused him.

Jesus looked at their frightened faces. He stood up, and said loudly, "Storm – be quiet!" Immediately the wind died, and the water became peaceful and calm once more. "Do you really trust me so little?" he asked them. "You should have known you were safe with me."

The disciples were amazed. "Just who is this man we are following?" they asked each other. "Even the wind and the waves obey him!"

Dead – or alive?

Jesus' enemies had won. His friends and family stood huddled together in the growing darkness. Above them hung the body of Jesus, on a cruel Roman cross. All their happiness, all their hopes, had ended with this.

Some of the Jewish leaders had been frightened of Jesus' power and popularity. They had tried to catch him doing something wrong. But instead, they had heard him criticizing the leaders, and teaching and healing the people in each town he came to. Hundreds of people cheered him as he rode into the city of Jerusalem. So his enemies had decided to get rid of him. And, with the Romans' help, they had succeeded.

Some of Jesus' friends laid his dead body in a cave in a quiet garden. They rolled a great rock over the opening and, feeling very sad, left him there.

All through the next day, the Sabbath, the disciples hid away. Would Jesus' enemies now hunt them out? They were miserable – and confused. They had seen Jesus do such wonderful things, and had learned so much from him. They had come to believe that he was the great leader God had promised, who would lead his people into freedom and joy. But now Jesus was dead.

Early next morning, Mary Magdalene, one of Jesus' friends, went to the tomb. She brought perfumes to pour over his body. She was worried about moving the huge rock which had been rolled across the opening to the tomb. But when she arrived, she saw that it had already been moved away. She rushed into the tomb: but Jesus' body was gone!

She hurried back to the disciples, and sobbed out her story. Then Peter and John ran to the garden. Inside the empty tomb, John realized that Jesus was alive. They rushed off to tell the others, leaving Mary behind, crying in the garden.

And then, a man spoke to her. "What's the matter?" he asked.

Mary peered at him through her tears. "Sir," she asked eagerly, "do you know where his body is?"

Then the man spoke her name. "Mary," he said.

When she heard his voice she knew who it was standing before her. "Jesus!" she cried, and her sadness turned into joy. He was alive!

Soon, Jesus had met all his friends and disciples again – and many other people, too. He came to Peter and to two friends walking home to Emmaeus. He came to his disciples as they hid in a locked room. Later he met them all on the beach and cooked them fish for breakfast.

Gradually, as they listened to Jesus and thought about all he had taught them before, the disciples learned what had really happened on that terrible day of his death.

They had thought Jesus' enemies had won. But they were wrong! Jesus' death had been part of a very special plan made by God right from the beginning of time.

"I had to die so that I could come back to life again," Jesus said. "God can now forgive all the wrong things done by people all over the world, for I was punished instead of them. Now, if anyone believes that I am God's son, and that I did this for them, they can become God's friends, and when they die they can live with me for ever. Your job is to tell this to everyone. But you will not have to do it alone. Remember all that I told you about the Helper I would send to you. The Holy Spirit will come soon and stay with you. He will teach and help you, as I have done."

And so Jesus left his disciples, and returned to his Father in heaven.